T0115168

God, I Wonder

INA M. EASTER

iUniverse, Inc.
Bloomington

God, I Wonder

iUniverse books may be ordered through booksellers or by contacting:

iUniverse
1663 Liberty Drive
Bloomington, IN 47403
www.iuniverse.com
1-800-Authors (1-800-288-4677)

Because of the dynamic nature of the Internet, any Web addresses or links contained in this
book may have changed since publication and may no longer be valid. The views expressed in
this work are solely those of the author and do not necessarily reflect the views of the publisher,
and the publisher hereby disclaims any responsibility for them.

ISBN: 978-1-4502-6662-8 (pbk)
ISBN: 978-1-4502-6664-2 (cloth)
ISBN: 978-1-4502-6663-5 (ebk)

Printed in the United States of America

iUniverse rev. date: 3/16/11

"My root is true, I'm open to spread the seed in life, the gifts & the joy in life that God planted and give to me".......................... Ina Easter

to the late: (AUNT & FRIEND):Barbara Breaux Noel Shelia
(Solomon) Sam somehow i wish you BOTH could see my words
onto this paper of white,... in black ink too; it's trully dynamite!!!"So
you know next one is off the chain; still by my name...",by:(I.M.E.-
+ZERO-)

Dedication

AS YOU KNOW GOD IS FIRST AMOUNT ALL THINGS IN
MY LIFE, HERE.......SECONDLLY I FIND MY CLOSE FAMILY
AND FRIENDS, SPECIAL UPROOTED LADIES SUCH
AS: AUNT-NANNY, CONNIE DAVIS, AUNT-NANNY,
ANNA SAM, MS.EVA S.,,PAULINE T., DIANA.C.,TWANA
S./E.,KAREN S./W.,DELORIA S.,TASHA S., LATOYA S.,
LOUISE ELINORA KELLY, MS. STACEY WOMACK, MS.
WOLFE, MS. DIANA, MS. BROUSSARD,MS DAWN, MS.
RACHEL, MRS. SONNIER, MS. MORGAN, MRS. RHONDA,
MS. DEVILLE, MS. PHILLIS, MRS. TRAHAN TO MANY
CO-WORKERS, WHOM MADE SURE I MADED IT TO
AND FROM WORK-(GOD BLESS YOU.....) AND FINALLY,
A GREAT AND WONDERFUL FRIEND, WHO BELIEVE
IN ME, AND HELP ME OVERCOME THINGS IN LIFE AS I
MOVE INTO IT........RIGHT,.....(MS. A. BOXIE).............

Contents

ABOUT ME....................

Well I'm one in a million that can say I got it well use it now, time is push and I won't be around to long to talk and see how wonderful my work play & the outcome it made here on earth........

Well, I was born Paterson, New Jersey, during the hot summer, August 04, 1969 where life was life, but yet I know I was to do God's calling so He blessed me with a great talent in life that speak out into my lines and drawing without a word from my mouth. I been thankful, as I put things He gave to me to use.....I came to Louisiana when I was nearly up and couldn't really understand what is my point in life, I watch and looked and seen how older people seen me. I seen how to move and when, where to go and when to stop and I founded my dream into the dark and little light...the light was the part in life that held me in and way from doing my best, above my best and to show my best to this world. I gave this life a good apart of me to hope one day it will pay the way back to me, but I seen I need to push and follow the road not make the road here......I try, and push and give in with a tear but no I believe more than what it was giving out to me so I continue and continue to express myself in church & newspaper.

Try to see if someone could hear or notice me...my luck came and it was beautiful time in and time out because we had little. No need to dream I believe, at this moment I could have but I couldn't. Time after time it when on like this and I wish and hope and pray and even try to win the lotto to get the money I need to continue my dream here on earth. Determination and little money, I mean a little money. I know no one could stop me not even me at this point in my life I got trier of believe what is reality if you don't feel it so I move into a new movement, but still I was poor living with a clean message from God, who listen anyway, no one because everyone's broke and looking for me to help them pay a bill until tomorrow, are maybe next week sometime.

Giving it all I got and I got it but a brick wall was built into my way, it wasn't man made at all because somehow I would had the strength to knock it down long time ago. So I put away the building block in life and start my own company call I can inside of me that was the dream that was the point into life I need to move toward the light in life I need. So as it was I did –I march from being just me to a true believe of hope love and understanding in life here. I gave God the weight and he taken it and allow me to walk like a butterfly into the air, my life became carefree, I didn't worry about things that I should, like have a door close into my face a friend to look down on my dream as a plan of unwanted passion in the wind. If anyone know me they known this was the begin of me not the end of my life, I'll tell anyone out there to never stop and move the way you want but just move. Your hopes are real go get it life ain't over when you want something, remember to keep your heart into it and live with the faith that what's your in life just go get it and don't be afraid to be put down, or turn around it's not the ending it the beginning of something new in life for you. Remember everyone felled in life, as a child you just didn't get up and walk from one corner of the house to another without a fall onto the floor. Take this into notion everyone have life and they the one to create the motion.

So place the rug out, and finish up, I learn that we all can, on this point I must say we will at one point in our life be who we want to be............

A View of Peace

Yesterday it rain
But today I write
Or type into the words
A upon the empty lines
I see something that
Appears so wonderful
To me. Something I
Had't had the change
To tell but today will
Makeup for yesterday
I lose the true color
as the sun reflected
back and reminded
me who is queen
Then the color of the
World that was hidden
Came out onto the
Trees top and falling
Leaves that cover the
Ground of green and
Made it appeared
To be gold just before
Me my fingers want
To grab and touch but
The soft wind blown
Against my coat and
Taken my eyes into
Far away place into
The open land where
Wild horses ran loosed
Into a pasture and old
Wheel barrel stood

As displace into the yard
And a road of quietness turn
Into a wooden fence
Ran around
The area of the
Land to nowhere
That I couldn't
Imaging or ever
Could say I been
I found this to
Be the most
Peaceful view
After taken off my
Shoes and place
Them into this body of water,
This claim lake.

I Ain't Did Nothing

Who blame me?
I ain't did nothing
Nothing, at all...
I'm just been sitting
Quietly and someone
Said, "She the one!"
But, I ain't did nothing....
Nothing, don't even known me,
And he don't even want no part of me,
Because I never cross his path or
Promise anything that I don't have
To give to nothing, that don't want no life to live
Don't bother me

I Am, Me!

No need to look into
Those books, or magazines
To find me,
I am, Me!
I am, not going put
On all that monkey's oil
Plan no plastic surgery
To change
No hair-piece, sew-in, are wear
woven-in-braided from human's hair,
Glued, wig or lock-in human hairs
Put on those painted pretty press —on
Nails, and wear those hand maded clothing
Costless colorful necklace
Of woven wooden bead
Or silver or golden link
Chain,
Slip on those mountain millionaire
Heels shoes
That make me stand so high
And so tall
Turning my Sundays best
Into junk clothing a bag or rags or less
Where people look at me and
As I walk into this unknown town
I want look out into this world
And walk with my head-up high
Not worry if it's O.K. to walk
Or pass this way because My-
Self-esteem may be low,
To low to have you look at,
Or unfold....

Old

Did I turn,
Or haven't I not yet learn
The style, of today
No way!
They said, "I am old!"
I just don't have it,
I can't keep up
I'm losing my step
Just beneath
I try to look away
And show them
They are wrong
I'm not old
I still could move
And perform as you,
Youngsters step
Into my move and
We'll see what
You all can do
I'm just moving,
Into my own steps
And following my
Own beat or tune

Do the World Cry?

I know, the world have eyes,
But doesn't the world cry?

Does the world feel my pain?
When I hurting over and over again...

I know, the world have eyes
For once I see the world
Turn the ice into tears, they cry
When the pain
Turn over inside of us all again,
When we all live then later, we die....

God Is Mines

I can't stop being excited about the way
Thing are going for me
I can't stop understand how wonderful
And blessing God has been to me.
I can't tell you the things that may make
Me cry to know how strongly
Jesus was on my side
I can't understand why
But I do wonder from day- to- day,
How come Jesus being so good to me
I can't understand why my devilish way
Don't scare him away
I can't understand
And may not never will
Why God
Just want to
Keep me close and
Hold me so near....

God I Wonder.....?

God I wonder.....?
Are you upset with me?
Are you please or disappointed in me?
Am I doing enough or not enough for you?
Can you understand me?
Do you understand me, Lord?
When I'm down and depressed
Or in need or sleep or little
Rest after long day
Lord, I could not be you
Or do your work as well
I'm not strong enough
Or faithful enough or caring
And loving as you

God Cry and I Pray

God sat to the corner of Heaven it
Seem as he was thinking thing over
I looked again, and I seen the tears that
Warm the earth's heart as it came
Down from his very eyes. I sat and
Looking but never could believe until I
Seen my Lord crying to Himself ... It touch me
What I have done? or what could I do to help
The greatest spirit of love of them all
Wipe up his tears I knee and say,
Thank you, Father for this day O my Lord
How I pray for all you have given
To me on this day. Thank you for giving
Me the strength to awake the ability
To go on the knowledge the understanding
The love protection of my children, family
And friend and the whole world as we began
This day a new and bless us as well into the
Ending of the night from all
Harm evilness and things of unrighteness, we
Love you Lord always forever and first you will
Remain our everything, as we carry around
This day...so the Lord look down on me
And smile as the tears he cried vanish
Away with brighten of light onto this day

Ladies Of Slaves

TO,
Ladies of slaves
Slaves of slaves
Slaves of the free ladies

Those, who got whipped
By the whip of whip makers
Wipe our eyes
Open up your eyes
Open up wide
Don't look away
Don't turn away
Don't you close your eyes yet
Can you see?
Do you believe?
Can't you believe?
The worst is not
The whip that
Lanch onto the board
Of your souls but the
Nails that wasn't pull out before the roots
Has gotten to old and hard
And gray like the nails
That maded their souls
Stood so long before it
Began to turn, wave in
Lend or bend into just
Above the earth but
Slowly, slowly, & slowly die

The ladies of the slaves
Slaves of slaves
Slave of free ladies
Today
Take your roots
Take your branches
Cut them
Look into
Look above
Look around
Don't stop
Don't forget
Don't be afraid
Open up
Speak
Write
Talk
March
Set into life
And live
Don't stop
Live
Don't stop
Remember
To march, walk, into life step by step
Open the doors!
Any door! Look, up; be proud......
(To be a root), a powerful root- a strong root
Of a lady, who use to be a slave
But now we live
With hope that tomorrow
Will be O.K.
Now we vote
For our true dreams, as we live and be proud,
Of the ladies that give us the wisdom to live
Our life so real and free

My Life Ain't So Bump

Lord
    I could almost cry,
To see my work of poetry
Turn into a book, into life,
I try to overcome and change
Things that are so wonderful, uplifting
Impressing to other folks.
They all look at the cover of my book
And walk on by
There's not a page they
want to read about
Me, my life ain't been so
Bump or bounce or
Even jumping everyday
Stand and reflect by
On just the same thing
Day after day
Lord,
    I asking for a new change
Of great wondering things to make me proud to sing
Truly how beatiful life have been to me

Stress

Somehow stress came inside
He really thought he caught me by surprise
I allow him to walk into my soul
He walk up down you know
Wondering what was wrong and what was right
But I think I know he didn't care if I hurted
He had my life turn, it upside down
My heart no longer feeling the time of need
To be here for life as you can see
He walk and wip my soul into pain
Lord, I am nervous and fill with shame
How I live like this
When you give me two fists to fight off my
Weakness in life
God, please come back and turn thing around
Before my life is no long found
On these ground on earth
Who would be standing in hurt
I sometime wondering inside
I have many tears to cry
Many stories to finish up and tell
I won't lie
I am in pain
As the blood runs down my viens
And my heart get to beat life into me
I known I was given another change to live
And be strong for God and me

I Just Want To Smile

Somehow, I see how people may hurt,
Live with pain broadcast on by other folks

How they go on after being call all type
Of foolish names.

I know the walk
But I can't talk

They print pages into my face,
When they look and
Stair at me as if they seen
Some type of ghost.

I cry like a baby and lower my head
Into my breast
I have no more hope I feel less

Of the image that God maded
I park my soul into the shade
And ask the light of day to beam
Another way

How come I looked so poor and ugly
But someone from nowhere
Said I like your smile it warm and true
I turn over and look and peek
At the sun
Try my best to be her friend again
So as she let her ray onto the earth
I turn and look up
At her and smile away

Jesus Is Everything

The world is beautiful
This, I know;
Jesus is everything
Everywhere I go
I see....
He is the plants,
He is the trees
He is life
He is me

Tomorrow I'll know
My wish will not be
To sail a kite into the skies
Or
Climb a tree so high
It will be for me to sit
Next to Jesus
Who's everything
Everywhere I go
He is the ocean
He is the lake
He is life
He is me

Jesus is everything,
Everything
I love to be

Some How I Am Happy

Somehow, I am happy if I hear from you
Talking over the telephone or good letter
Of hope from you
Some how I am happy most to see your
Feeling O.K.
I'm alright but my life is not complete
Without you
Somehow, I am happy to know the faith we
keep brought us out of the wood and
into the light of tomorrow,
tomorrow, will see how happy I'll be when I'm standing
Right next to you!

With a Promise of Hope

With the promise of hope,
That tomorrow will not be in vain
They'll grow health with your name
I walk on, not run!
Toward light, that morning's sun
Facing Jesus with a tender smile
How happy He is to see after all those miles
I sat into His kingdom's seat
Everything is beautiful as they told it to me
I tough the rose that capture my eyes
As an angel with wings pass me by
My trouble of the world, I known as earth will be all over
As my tears wash my face
I woke from my dream I'm back on earth again
Where I face another day of trouble rain
But I'm carrying Jesus as my weapon
Against it to prove I'm not afraid
To walk this land

My Last Day on Earth

There's nothing like the smell of the opening wildflowers,
Walking through the wandering, wild crispy fall's leaves of winter
Colors,
Of rainbow country countless of the golden- brown fur backs of
Squirrels run up and down the yearly oak beautiful bark trees airplane
Passing by into the clouds, they disappear,
Listening to the birds chuttring songs of grace, up lift from nowhere a
Precious wanted beautiful banana butterfly dancing on your loose
Finger tips watch the trees talk sign language in which no one but they
Care
The evening's winds blow leaves into the greenish-brown ground and
Slowly spreading them all about

Watching a child with no knowledge challenge
His world of hope and new dreams
To open the door to opportunities, that allow everyone a space to
Breath
To see more love from this world cast above into the hearts of man
To sweep the rug of violence and let it's dust vanish and never return
Into noone view
Keep the faith, the truth about God stand as all man must come to face
These open gates

My last days, will be pleased with joy & with a smile
He'll touch me, with opening arms, I'll run into
Lift my head, to (Jesus), at once I'm there..No
        Look below
Onto earth where I once lived
To appreciated the joy the love that now God have
To give to me, his true life of forever faith indeed
Is now the road I'll see

A Corner View

My eyes hidden into the corner of the room
Looking at the beautiful flowers that bloom
Across the old wooden table top was place an arrangement of
flowers
Into a crystal vase
As I stood by I could see a picture of
A family that live in this house
They call home- a place

Slim Lady

A slim tall black lady
In jean with heels looking
Mean. Pull out a cigar
From her purse into her
Mouth she lit it up and
Puff on it and blown out
Some smoke, as she
Cross the busy street swinging
Her bags away into a
Distant she went and went about her way

You Give Me a Pen

How come I write?
How come the world must know?
What's makes me happy when I'm sad?
What make me weak to my knees?
What promise lays ahead?
You gave me a pen!
I wrote,
Little by little
Into notes
Hoping you'll understand me
Did I speak clear?
Did I reach your inner ear?
That tomorrow is real
Did you lose it somewhere
Down there?
Between the line
You better catch up it's an open line
I know you have what it take to reach- out to me
And tell me the pen you gave ran out of ink
That ends of this story to you from me.

My Child

How many times we sat and talked,
Mama only wanted you to walk
The path of righteousness and peace
Please, pull yourself from off those streets
I'm getting all sick inside
And it's a shame if I cry!
The neighbors say I am going down the drain,
But my child, it's you who cause my pain
You stay going all night
Until the morning light
You know you got no job
Those white folks looking for you—did you rob
That Shell station down the street
Where I used to get my cigarettes and sweets,
Made money orders to pay my bills
And bought all my needed pills?
You'd better answer me before I hit you upside your head
And they'll be along our street talking about what they read.
Mama can't take no more headaches
It's all on me, your mistakes
Your daddy, he ain't got no time to be seeing you in jail
He's too busy working hard for his new family; can't you tell?
He ain't paid me a child support check in years
And I'm supposed to talk to him, in his ear
And ask him for something?
He knows what I need and what he needs to do
I'm tired of wearing these old, banged-up work shoes
To church on Sunday.
Fighting those bills and living, it kills me.
Maybe if you get a part-time job, instead,
Change your life, child, and comb your head
And look decent in front of those folks.

Then maybe we could see some strong hope—
For you and your tomorrows
I truly believe they'll be filled with sorrow.
I look at all your friends; they all look doped up and high,
They all look in another direction—can't look you in the eye.
By the way, your old girlfriend called up here
Saying she's pregnant, and you may be the father!
What's wrong, son? Where did I go wrong?
I gave you everything I had,
And at this point in my life, it's sad.
You were too busy running with knives and guns;
You think you're an outlaw, or gangster.
You'd better walk and talk to Jesus and tell Him to be on your side
You're going to need more than a prayer at this point, I cry,
My child that used to look toward the stars in the skies
Now his heart is looking far away into life
He's walking fast into the world he calls hope and peace
But as his mama, I still falling down onto my knee
Every night and calling out to the Lord, to please
Take my child, Lord—my only child from those streets
Amen!

My Life Fell In

I watch into the distance,
I turn around and there it ends.
No more pathway,
No more life,
No more dreams I had to fight.
Before the light,
My life fell into his hands.
I do not belong on this land
To see
To live
To enjoy
This place any more.
But as I live and live right,
Into evening, after the
Rainbow sets and sunset melts
Before I could imagine
Your going, beyond the evening moon.

O Africa

O Africa, O Africa,
Awake and rise
Before the hot sun lifts her head.
Can you feel the earliness in your bones?
Life for the poor black mom
Means wake up, no sleep, you have plenty of work to do,
Beat the darkness, race before he turns light
Break before your work is done.

If

If I could let you read these words
That were promised to me,
I know I'd no longer
Have something that
You wanted to hear.
You would not be amazed by me,
So I close this book
And I look another way,
Pretend that I don't
Hear you call,
Asking me to stay.
So if I just let you,
I wonder if you'll come
Back tomorrow.
As I push today away from your view
On what I have to say,
Then I may tell you to come see me tomorrow
And play those same old games.

A Move

From one day to another,
My ancients tried so hard to move
Between desegregation lines, they froze their roots.

A man know his boundary,
A man lives to see his rightness in life.
A child cries,
The telephone rings
The front door's bell automatically sings.
But nothing brings back a man's freedom that costs
The strength to stand up for what he believes in.

If I could give life,
I'd give, not take.
I'd move forward and
Unfold things with people who just don't want to open up,
Bother with, or are afraid to talk
And fight about.
I want to walk in the shoes
Of those ancients—years of great passion and unrooted pain,
Once again, live their cries inside.
Our country is truly blessed,
Our lives are great.
Our memories are dried, folded, and put away into a locked
drawer.
The picture turns from black and white into color glosses,
The pathway to move the dream, look into my face.

We move to new challenges, directions, and things,
We, holding hands, complete a rainbow.
We paint this world once again,
I am proud to walk with a smile.

A man's dream is a dream of his life and all he'll live,
Building faith and a strong belief in Christ.
Between each disappointment, he'll cry.
Between his happiness, he'll find room to celebrate
This great moment in life.
But between each movement, he'll stop hoping
And look over what he's done in his life.
Usually it's not enough, so he'll just move and move on,
Trying so hard to make it better or right
For those who may see nothing and reply, he just lived his life.

They Stood

Somehow my walk down the street
Became more fulfilling.
Along a healthy dark-brown broken bark
Of a golden orange, brightly highlighted, yellowish chestnut maple,
Came a brownish, furry little thing,
With pop-out eyes that saw everything,
Little hands filled with twigs and broken vine.
I walked up to him with heavy steps,
He looked at me as if I was one of them.
I wanted him to run and go away.
He stood his ground with amazing grace,
He stood me down from head to toe,
Watched me act to interrupt his path,
Down came the uninvited friend
Who stood with his deep eyes looking into mine.
Somehow, I couldn't get them to run or go,
Two furry, brownish squirrels stood around
And watched me until I got on my bus that carried me to town.

A Broom

A ladylike,

Wooden frame,

Handle long and slim

With ring nose,

Straight straw hair

That may bend,

Sweep across the open,

Hand-made wooden floors.

Pick up things that

Leave your house looking messy.

Tomorrow

is just a step away,
So close your eyes and let's all pray
The tenderness of the clouds fall
And awaken us all into the new day,
For which we all are truly looking for.

Smile

Some say it opens up the hearts

And lightens the soul.

I find a smile is greater

Than opening up a window for fresh air.

I watch a baby smile,

Then an old man,

Then a lady who didn't speak English to me.

But I put on a beautiful smile that

Spelled out, "I'm your friend too."

Change

The darkness overcast the evening skies,
A lone girl, who cries
Into the wind,
A mother with a wish of hope again,
That her child embrace his fist of faith,
And let the world see his life has changed.
He's now a believer of hope, do away with his wrong.
He is willing to stand and show all that he now is,
Strong, he is willing to change as he bends
Down onto his knees and asks God to forgive him
For all of his sins,
And give him a new change in life as it begins.

Remembering a Moment

The sounds of pouring rain,
Thunder, lightning it's flood bank again.

Day of sunshine and great light heat waves,
Dancing and bouncing into the view around,

Bees, flies, and mosquitoes try to get the best of me.

Lazy daisies, dried up roots, broken branches,
An old man cutting it all between his green grass lawn.

Smell of cigarettes, trash burning, someone
Cooking oak gumbo with chicken & sausage, and muddy
Brown stew. Barbecue pits set off
Flames dancing into the wind.
Christmas's tree spreading the smell of
Fresh pine cones.

A holy church bell ringing at seven, a train passing.
A child who is learning how to ride his two-wheeler bike
Falls and gets back on without a cry.

I check the mailbox. No mail, good news.
One day away from worrying about bills
That I must pay before
The weekend,
And bend over and turn before me.

Jesus (Don't Owe Us Anything)

Wow! Are you amazed with your life? This your perfect gift, which Jesus gave to all of us. He doesn't owe us anything. We must worship and praise him for his precious form of art. Remember how he blew wind into life into us, into his great ideal of imagination, his formation, his lovely creation. How come we sit back, relax, act lazy, refuse to work in this world and give it all we've got for once? Why do we think he owes us something for being here, upon this muddy ground (of no return). As we carry our sinful soul into the edge of his valley, we watch the light beam, and then turn up our noses continually to walk away, as if we don't need, or have no business here. But we're wrong to look down upon our maker, our creator as if he's nothing or he's never been here for us. I believe time is too beautiful to be hiding his spirit of glory behind, beyond those rocky mountains on earth. Jesus has better things for all of us. Jesus don't owe us anything. May I say he gave life as a present, now sit down and open it, unwrap it, and enjoy it, as we learn to appreciate and love what he gave us (life).

Colored Folks

Colored folks,

Open up the doors,

Stop your sleepin',

Awake into life.

Look ahead, beyond, and above

Those clouds; bypass

Those stars, and that faded,

Old dusty, rusty, and golden moon.

There it goes, like a soft bubble and a faithful wish,

An angel of hope,

With wings of justice for us all.

I Ain't Mad

I try to smile into your face,
I don't think you care
To see my face.
I let off some steam,
I take it, pour it into my coffee-n-cream.
The television is filled with latest news,
You turn away and don't look at me,
Are you still blue?
I ain't mad.
With you, I could live like this,
You and I will not fight with our fists.
We can't take this relationship into a rage,
No one wants to land on the first page.
The world don't need to know about our expressions,
Take time out, that's my suggestion.
If you're mad, it's OK to be,
But you must remember this—
It's not just your life, you're now with me.
Our kids are moving up into life,
They know how I love being your wife.
Do you want to walk? Do you want to talk?
Please make up your mind,
The clock is moving into time.
It's great to know you're no longer stressed or mad.
I'm here to love,
You look away and forget about the pass.
You see what a little cooling off can do?

Look

Look through my semi-smile
And tell me do you know
What I'm thinking, what's on
My mind?
Do I have anything to tell you,
Or the world as well.
As I look into the lens
Of the camera and smile for a
Moment to give you a smile
That will last a lifetime in a frame,
Unname!
So folks can pass and see
One moment, one memory of me,
Just as happy as a baby.
They'll look and smile away
As if I'm there to smile back and say
Have a wonderful day.

If I Could Stay

If I could stay
Just this way,
What would my mother say?
She'd be pleased
To have her dreams
Of me being sweet.
I know I'll grow
And change
Into other flowers
Of arrangement
That may open up her
Nose and ears.
I'll surprise her with
My life, of open clear
Blue clouds that just
Pass then go.
She'll be pleased with my roots,
My growth.
After all, a plant
Can't stay one way.
It must branch outward
And find its way.
That why, Mother, I'll
Remember all your planning
And walk
Right into this world,
My life, and be like a
Bee and stand out
And give all I've got
To be the greatest.

Mirror into My Apartment

The sun ran down into the middle of the city, sweeping leftover broke up
Rays into the heaven, thick clouds of the fresh windy afternoon
Traffic into the land. People walking home into working busy street sounds
blown in and out,
Children shout all about,
Playing games into life before the day becomes darken and heavy, thick and black,
Where wildlife appears between each bark.
I sit against my window to continue to view
Into my mirror life, reflect an image of me and you.
If you could see something in me that you want,
Something special, open and don't stop there, come to see me.
I'm just sitting and watching life come into view
—a land beyond my eyes; I can't picture being with you.
But as this day dances into its resting nest,
I find a life of hope in its best,
A reflection into the mirror view,
From my high apartment building where I stay and find life worth living,
Where my heart is the tool for giving,
Anything that reflect back to me is truly my life, hope, not a dream.
So if you don't appreciate your image,
Turn your life into form or reflect toward a new attitude
Of about who is who
When you look into mirror at you.

Anyway . . .

If a beautiful wild cherry could be me
It would be no sweeter to you. Believe me,
I'm a real, rooted lady, shadowed in my loneliness,
Hoping for the right gentleman to give
Me a new life, deepen my wish, walk in the pathway,
Enter into God's precious dew where we can be as one.
But if you don't see my dream, or can't fullfill my wish,
I'll take next bus out … hopefully, I'll find some way
Or any way to end all of this.

When She Spoke

I heard some voices talking in the wind.
Slowly their echoes rose above the wall that was so thin,
Their disappointments overlapped with the dissatisfaction
That was displayed in the woman's open speech.
She spoke above and loud and so deep,
She told of a cry that brushed against her,
She said the cry was planted; now it was overgrown.
It wants to live and be free.
How could they stand up like me?
She asked the sun for her light
And begged the clouds for their tears (bring forward the rain)
To keep this might soldier brave and strong.
His faith lay between
Those grounds of weeds.
The faith was released as he built within,
And he had to live with it,
Not turn against it,
Try to continually look back on it,
Sweep into it,
Rise with it,
Go for it,
Be with it.
For once he could appreciate his life as it blew like a breeze,
For once his life felt like hope,
He was carefree above the clouds into the wind
Like an airplane, he'd taken off,
Sailed slowly and softly against the claim lake—into a ship,
Carrying his determinations onto a speeding train.
He'll never look back. He must go
To a life that is now his own
He passes
But doesn't stop above or on this green grass.

Oh, Ladies (Here's Our Hope!)

I use to live,
What for?
H.O.P.E.
For once, I'll try
To be ...
True
Strong
Fresh
Free
Independent
Responsible.
I'll take the keys in life
And make them real
So they can live
As you and me.
So positive
Willing
Open to life
I'll let them be
All they can be.
I release them
To the open
To be free
To make their own
Decisions.
The only things in life
That make me so
Proud
Joyful
Overwhelmed
Outgoing
Brave

Independent
Reliable
Faithful
And
True.

Pass a Year

The year began
Like an open flower
Of spring, new and true
To my heart …

As the summer's sun
Climbs upward into open
Bright sky and shines,
I find a lot of things
That my ten fingers alone
Can do beside the waters.
How about fishing with
Grandpa for once—is it
All right by you?

Between the rainbow and crispy
Falling leaves I follow
My own footsteps into my own dreams
And passing tomorrow as it fades away,
Making room for me to live today.

Somehow the smoothness of
The smokey mountaintops
Covered in layers of
Snow white ice turn my
Nose like a rose of
Sweet maple brown
Syrup. How I've been taken
Away by one of God's
Heaven's flakes. How
Beautiful, I must
Admit, to all of this.

Hey, Shadow

Every moment
Looks about the same.
You appear to be gray
Or dark gray but you
Look a lot bigger
Than me.
You never seem to
Miss one step, react,
Or lose control of anything
That I plan to do.
You're sort of like a
Copycat, but you're
A friend to me,
Because you have
No mouth to tell
Anyone my secrets after
The light is gone ...
And you're not there
Tracing my steps and my
Moments over and over again.

Red Robin

Red Robin,
Red Robin,
In a tree

Red Robin,
Red Robin,
Callin' for me.

Red Robin,
Red Robin,
When you blow
Into my ear

Red Robin,
Red Robin,
I know you
Sing a sweet
Love song just for me,
To let me
know you're in the nearby trees, waiting
To come out and be amazed and see ...

Hummingbird

Between the fanning leaves of green,
Way up high along the arms
That branch into that tree
Of oak, sat a singer ...
A maker,
An everlasting note taker
Of words, that could be heard in tunes.

Of the hummingbird's calling of notes
That are sweeter than ice cream,
Caramel and green apple; because
It seems too relaxing to my inner
Ears and takes my mind away
Into another peaceful and
Wonderful and lovely place.

When I Wrote

Sometimes I wrote plain or about things
Upon an old piece of white paper,
A magazine cover, on the side of cereal boxes,
The inner lining of hardcover books,
An old crisp brown paper bag,
Or a label or a tag,
In crayons on the hallway walls,
Upon the refrigerator with eraseable
Markers …
When I wrote,
It was good,
It was real,
It was for a cause,
Something I had to say
Before someone else could. I race,
Now I am in place,
I am first
To say these things. Listen …

A Black Woman

black woman's soul is tender;
It's more tender when it's
Held, loved, and warmed.

A black woman smiles
When she's treated with a gift
That spells "I love," even
Once in a while.

A black woman has
Dreams and stands alone
But she prefers a man
With a machine gun
That's built like a bone.

Pretty Black Seed

Roots
Grown into, I could never be
Mistaken for a slice of
Cooked, golden brown bacon,
Golden crispy fried chicken, baked
Potato or baked beans, sweet,
Soft brown roll, tender roasted
Or med-cooked steak upon anyone's
Plate. I'm a pretty, shiny, black
Seed that grew up. Well and pretty,
Onto this land, looking out onto life
To see where opportunity pours
Like water and runs right toward
Me, and shines his golden sun's
Ray of light once again for me.

Talk Too Much

Hey!
Am I
Talking a little too much?
Do you want me to shut up?
Before I finish telling
You what should be or not,
I can end, but I know you'll
Think something is wrong
With me. So, I would like
To continue after all of
This but this damned pen
Is about to run out of ink
On me ...
($3.00)

Sounds

Listen, onto the earth there go the wonderful sounds
Spinning and turning all around,
As you went into nature, the wild monkeys
Called out to one another from tree to tree.
Mosquitoes, bees, dragonflies, and beetles
Busily working everywhere. I took a moment
And stole away nature, wild, where I saw
Life open up like the sun's rays and the
Sound of life spread over into the uprooted trees,
Fulfilling the ground.

I Will Not Follow

I will not follow—
Because I am a leader,
I am top director,
I am professor,
I am impresser.
I will show and tell,
Live strong and well,
Touch any mountaintop or hill.
I know books,
Not page by page,
Thou people's expression of outrage.
I will not follow
Into those shoes,
But play by my own rules,
Live according to what is real,
And teach the truth. Show my daughters not to steal.
Open up your dreams, set aside your play toys,
Sweep up you life, do away with boys
Until your roots are strongly in place.
Don't turn and step on my feet as I am wrong,
I want you walk proud,
Wipe those soft tears from your eyes.
Remember, life is a gift. Don't misuse it at all,
Because you'll be turned back between your falls.
I will not follow
Into anyone's traces
No one will watch my back
As I walk into open view
With no one to tell me what to do.
I am living prove
That a black woman can stand (in this world)
And live and not be afraid

Of anything that she must face,
Just a thing that she can overcome.
She stands truly above them all
Without being a shadow,
That dark and gray that comes out between light
And open sun rays.
She stands upon her own two feet,
Lady, you want to be grown,
Remember not to follow but to lead,
Give life your knowledge and let the world believe.
Let them see you continue to fly
Above
Don't give up, don't cry.

Just pray with love
And step into life above those roots
Where is your favor booth.
So you may be seen
As a shining star of well-being.
Remember your head
Is your guiding point,
So go on … and live now,
And face the storm.

Ladybug

Ladybug in a tree
How beautiful you are to me.
I want to take you into my hand
And carry you away,
But I know nature needed you
More than I did today,
So I let you be
As you moved so slowly
Up the bark of that tree.

Brother, Thanks to You

Brother,
You led the way,
You held my hands as we played,
We played catch and a little baseball
With a few others, I recall.
You showed me how to swing, how to hit,
You showed me how to keep up my guard
When I was alone.
You made me a strong youth, but now
I am fully grown.
Between everything, like oaks' branches and dirt,
You told me to wipe my tears, be brave,
And not to show my hurt.
Brother, this is to you for you goodness to
Me in life,
How you kept me on the road of righteousness
And toward the light.
Now I am grown into the perfect lady inside,
Who sees life so beautiful with nothing
To hide, so I walk proudly into the crowd.

Being Black

Who knows me?
Beside the outer covering of my skin
They tell me I'm black and I haven't always been free,
They tell me to look into my life, plant my seed,
Stand up for what I believe.
Don't stop my dreams,
Always place my faith in my vote,
Live with strong a will in my hands of hope.
Drinking from different fountains is our past,
Can you hear bells of freedom at last?
Our children are playing in rainbow
And my face touches the breeze.
God I thank you. I know you're pleased.
Being black isn't so bad,
I can't see why color ruins
So many people's lives. That's sad.

Believing

There is a change,
A time—
A place to believe
In all that is not really real.
I want to see things come to the light,
Light come to live,
Hope open and open into a new front door.
I want it so that ladies become winners in life,
With things that set us apart from men.
Ladies, take over, take a step,
Open your windows to life.
Break a plate before it's too late,
Drink at the well, uncover the secrets
That they never tell.
Stop making and believing just believe
In all your opportunities, and do
Put away those fake dreams.
Give your life, you, before it
Turns to dust, is worthless
And overdue, like a library book.

Boys in Stone

Where is your life gone,
In a wall of stone?
Who will pay the price
When you roll the dice?
It's hard to said how you feel
When you know you're not living life so real.
You choose the fast lane,
You know those boys ain't playin' games.
They go hard into life,
Drinking and smoking those drugs. That's illegal and it ain't right.
Your pathway could be broken now
If you just turned around.
Give your life to Christ,
He'll make you feel all right.
Between your days of praying,
There're many things you have to say.
I want to see you live,
I don't want see you give
Your life to the street.
It's hard out there, you see.
If you don't understand,
Please grab onto my hands
And let me take you for a walk,
And we can have a talk,
And I'll show you the boys in stones
Who lived fast lives of joy, but now they gone.
Some of them are your friends,
Faces you may not remember, whose lives have ended.
I hope and trust you'll stay,
Instead of walking away
Into the dark,
Into an unwanted park,
And closing the door
To your life forever.

Don't Give Up

Cops running in and out of the valley,
Down into dark, dirty, and creepy alley.
A murder just taken place—young girl
In her twenties, they could see blood running down her face.
She just walked home from work,
Didn't do any harm to anyone, she never hurt.
Some old drug user in need
Decided to take advantage of her, you see
He wanted to feed
His brain with that weed and dope,
He found his wishes, he found his hope
Fighting for her purse.
She was a student, a waitress, and a nurse.
God knows he didn't have to take her life,
She planned a future, a lady in white.
Her parents are drowning in tears,
Hoping this man get life, not a couple of years.
He's facing them in court with his head down in his hands,
Her mother crying, my child is gone, no longer walks upon this land.
And you think she'd have the heart to set him free?
He'll never live that day of light to see
Between frames of pictures is new life.
She's open to Jesus Christ with faith,
She gains the hope, the strength to not give up now on life,
Turns to and talks to the spirit of hope who makes it right.

It Takes a Lot of Work

It takes a lot of work
To get what you want in life,
To get what is yours,
To take what belongs to you,
To face this world over
Again with your hand up
Into air because you don't
Want to fight.

It takes a lot of work
To be on top,
To iron out the bends and folds,
To walk straight into the road,
To give life the time to shine against your shoulder blades,
And ride into life with a positive hope and strong rays,
Turn broken glass
Into solid rock
To lean against wall of building blocks,
Turn a bully
Into a dreamer of life
During your falls,
Turn your favorite blue jeans
Into a new adventure made of soy beans.

It takes a lot of work
To build this house
Into a home,
To build this bridge
Into an overpass for the main road,
To build a small city
Into a classic place,
To build tiny fingers

Into perfect tools,
To build a long, dependable
Dream of your life,
Worship into Christ
It takes a lot of work,
But it must be done.
Your have won,
Remember, it took alot of work to get done

The following poems was added to my book, because I feel to believe what we do in life reflect our children; and as they grow and learn here. So to all parents out there, be all you can so your offspring would be better. Remember they are the future and it began with us..........

This poem was written by asia solomon when she was in the 3rd grade with a little help here..., Her poem took to life............

What Are Moms For? By: Asia Solomon

Moms, they care about others;
Moms are there when your sick.
I don't know about your mom,
But, my mom is kind.....
She always thankful,
She always doing things
And she laugh about stuff,
But what she laughing about?
I don't know?
I know she is happy!

All moms are great about
Caring
Loving
Being kind
Thankful
And sweet to us all....
So to you, mom
Have a blessing mother's day.

The following poem was written by precious, who rather a field of law...But that's still ok by me.

Sunday's Afternoon By: Precious Solomon

Sunday's afternoon,
My grandma and i
Cooked a turkey breast;
To much to season,
To much to cut
Hours of pepreation, but
Soon it will be done.
We sat the glass table,
And put the flowers in the center.
We turned the fire down, and sang song
After lighting a candle,
We held hands ,
To say our grace....
Dinner was served!
Afterward,
I'm feeling full
Then,
I'm feeling tired
Napping on the couch
In the light of the moon...
I dream of our
Next big feast.